Amen

Seeking Presence
with Prayer,
Poetry,
and Mindfulness
Practice

Amen

Seeking Presence
with Prayer,
Poetry,
and Mindfulness
Practice

RABBI
KARYN D. KEDAR

CENTRAL CONFERENCE OF AMERICAN RABBIS
New York · 2020/5780

Names: Kedar, Karyn D., 1957– author.
Title: Amen : seeking presence with prayer, poetry, and mindfulness
    practice / Rabbi Karyn D Kedar.
Description: New York : Central Conference of American Rabbis, 2020. |
    Summary: "This collection includes prayers for personal use, prayers for
    use at communal gatherings, prayers and readings for moments of grief
    and moments of joy, a collection of daily Psalms, and focus phrases and
    questions for meditation"—Provided by publisher.
Identifiers: LCCN 2019039152 | ISBN 9780881233506 (paperback) | ISBN
    9780881233513 (ebook)
Subjects: LCSH: Judaism—Prayers and devotions. | Spiritual life—Judaism.
Classification: LCC BM665 .K53 2020 | DDC 296.4/5—dc23
LC record available at https://lccn.loc.gov/2019039152

Text design and composition by
Scott-Martin Kosofsky
at The Philidor Company,
Rhinebeck, NY

CCAR Press, 355 Lexington Avenue, New York, NY 10017
(212) 972-3636
www.ccarpress.org
Printed in the U.S.A.
10 9 8 7 6 5 4 3 2 1

To my father

Norman Dion Schwartz

July 10, 1928–January 10, 2016

because of you

Acknowledgments

WITH HUMILITY and an open heart, I offer gratitude to my teachers of mindfulness practice from the Institute for Jewish Spirituality and spiritual direction from the Bekhol Levavkha Training Program: Rabbi Lisa Goldstein, Cantor Richard Cohen, Rabbi Jonathan Slater, Rabbi Myriam Klotz, Rabbi David Adelson, Dr. Barbara Breitman, and my study partners Rabbi Lisa Grant, Rabbi Nancy Wiener, Juliet Spitzer, as well as all my colleagues in both cohorts. For four years during both of these cohorts, I was in the presence of brilliance, grace, and curiosity. This book would have been different without your teaching.

Congregation B'nai Jehoshua Beth Elohim (BJBE) has invested in my learning and writing with joy and graciousness. Throughout sixteen years you have said to me over and over, "Go and study, and come back and teach us what you have learned." And you asked me on a regular basis, "Are you writing a new book? We look forward to reading it." The leadership of BJBE is kind, visionary, and brave. I am so honored to serve this beautiful congregation.

To my clergy team, Cantor Jennifer Frost, Cantor Rayna Green, Rabbi Jason Fenster: We celebrate one another all the time. You lift me higher. Thank you for creating a culture of support, inspiration, imagination, excellence, and serious growth.

Leslie Block: Ninja! Nothing happens without you. You have become a dear friend and an indispensable support.

Lindsay Griseta: In the morning service the prayer for the

body precedes the prayer for the soul. Your joy, laughter, and skill have kept me healthy and strong.

To Rabbi Hara Person and her entire team, including Rabbi Sonja Pilz, Sasha Smith, Ortal Bensky, Debbie Smilow, Rabbi Dan Medwin, and Raquel Fairweather: You continually provide the platform where ideas and creativity can flourish. This is an enduring gift to the Jewish people. I am grateful to you for encouraging me to write and including my work on your shelf.

To my family: Ilan, you were a great writing partner in the cafes of Tel Aviv. Talia, Shiri, and Ilan, it is my privilege and delight to talk ideas, philosophical questions, and the mysteries of the human spirit with you.

Shiri, Omri and Leo, Talia, Moti, and Lihi, Maya, Eliyah, Emma—love you so . . . and to Ezra, who makes it all possible, love is the context for it all.

Lynore Schwartz: Mama bear, the Queen Mother, Ma, you are the very definition of unconditional love.

Contents

vii Acknowledgments

xv Introduction

Section I: Awakening the Spiritual Path

3 Bearing Witness

4 Beholden

5 Tumble Prayer

6 Only This

7 God of Mercy

8 All Is Possible

9 I Wake Before the Dawn

10 Call Upon Me

11 Waiting

12 Resilience

13 The Archaeologist of the Soul

15 Whispers

16 At Some Point We Wake

17 Humility

18 Lift Me: A Morning Song

19 Quiet My Soul, O Holy One

20 Trust

21 Meaning

22 Learning

23 Decide

24 Always Mortal

26 Fear and Hope

27 Presence

28 Supplication

30 Repentance

31 The Creative Spirit

32 Learning to Yield

34 Stretch Out Your Light

35 Loss Is a Cleansing

36 Love

37 Turn to the Light

38 Resolve

39 To the God of Enigma

41 Light and Dust

42 Choosing

43 Atonement

45 Hope Is the Bridge

46 Hold Me in Prayer

47 The Ghost of Love

48 Overflow: The Prayer of the Well Digger

50 Guide Me

51 Hide and Seek

52 Return

53 Abundance

54 My Rock

55 Give Away the Pain

56 Perpetual Crossings

57 A Simple Awareness

58 Doubt

59 Courage

60 Build a Vessel of Compassion

61 God of All Things

62 Life Defined

63 Open My Eyes

64 Discern

65 To the Morning God

66 Forgiveness

67 A More Gentle Voice

69 The Truth

70 Hope, Banish My Despair

71 A Nighttime Prayer

73 Presence

74 To the God of Another Day: A Song

75 Linger

76 Wonder

77 In Between

79 To the Uplifting God: Help Me

81 Ordinary Splendor

82 Amen

83 Imagination

84 Make of Me a Vessel

86 To the God of Simple Elegance: Hallelujah

87 Gratitude

88 Release Me

89 Joy

Section II: God's Tears

GRIEF AND MOURNING

95 Dying: To the God, Who Teaches

97 *Esa Einai*: I Lift My Eyes

99 Learning from Death

100 From a Mother to Her Girls

102 For My Father

104 To the God of Mystery

105 *Kaddish*: You Ask So Much

106 *Yizkor*: Remember

108 The Valley

ACTS OF VIOLENCE, WAR, AND NATURAL DISASTER

111 For Courage and Comfort

113 To the God of Doubt

114 A Prayer of Courage and Consolation

115 For the Children
116 Restore What Is Broken
117 For Suffering
118 To the God of Creation

PRAYERS OF PEACE AND MEMORIAL

121 Light and Warmth
122 A Prayer for Nonviolence
123 Blessing for the Soldiers
124 In Time of War in Israel: A Prayer for Courage
125 For Those Who Serve and Defend: We Remember
126 Israel Memorial Day

Section III: Our Common Purpose: Prayers for Community and Assembly

129 The Call to Service
130 The Covenant of Leadership
131 The Leadership Pledge
132 A Blessing for Our Community
133 For the Women of the Wall: Hear Our Prayer
135 A Prayer for an Assembly
136 A Prayer for a Community Gathering
137 A Prayer for Justice and Democracy
138 A Convocation for an Interfaith Gathering

Section IV: The Psalm of the Day

141 Sunday: Psalm 24
     To God of the Heights: Lift Me
142 Monday: Psalm 48
     To the God of War and Peace: Prevail
143 Tuesday: Psalm 82
     To the Judge of All the Earth: Advocate
144 Wednesday: Psalm 94
     To the God of Peace: Save Us

145 Thursday: Psalm 81
     To the God of Creation: A Song of Thanks
146 Friday: Psalm 93
     To the Center of the Universe: A Yielding
148 The Sabbath: Psalm 92
     A Song of Gratitude: Open My Heart

Section V: Focus Phrases
155 Finding Meaning and Purpose
159 Guidance
163 Self-Love
167 Forgiveness
171 Positive Energy
175 Courage

Section VI: Questions
183 Faith
184 Courage
185 Wisdom

187 *Notes*

Introduction

IT WAS RAINING, with thunder and lightning. The kind of downpour that wakes you up. The time was 2:00 a.m. For a brief second, I was in awe of the power of the rain and the heavenly sound and light show.

And then I was annoyed.

"Not so hard!" I thought. "Not so fierce! The ground is too dry to absorb all this blessed rain. . . . Did I even fill the sump-pump battery with distilled water? . . . Stop, I tell you, or the basement will flood!" And then, in proper responsive-reading form, the rain took its cue and picked up. There was a powerful rupture of clouds and, despite my pleas, a more insistent pelting of rain. "The flights!" I thought. "My afternoon flight will be delayed, or even worse, it will be canceled. Stop, please stop." What began as my indignant tone was deteriorating into a resignation and a whimper.

It went on like that for quite a while—the prayer of the heavens, the protest of my heart—until finally I rose from my bed, agitated, and again the rain seemed to respond. But this time, it was different. The rain suddenly stopped, and there was silence. That was it. No more rain. A break in the clouds.

As the sun began to rise, the night giving way to the light, I pondered the meaning of "amen."

How often do we awake with a sense of awe and well-being, only to have it dissipate in moments?

Prayer helps us linger in the blessing.

I remember that when I was a child, I asked my father the meaning of "amen." "It means 'me too,'" he told me. And so I believed and taught without question for many years.

As I grew older and the prayers of others surrounded me—prayers of people in trouble, in distress, people who were afraid or sick or whose loved one was sick—I realized it is not always easy to say "amen." After all, sometimes prayer is wordless, a simple nod or resigning shrug of the shoulders. And sometimes prayer is ugly—an angry fist shaking at the heavens or an audible sigh from the depths of the gut. How do we respond to that type of prayer?

Amen. Me too.

The truth is, sometimes "amen" is just about the *only* response that could possibly encompass the complexity of everything we feel: resistance, impatience, protest, resignation, joy, wonder, and even confirmation. And sometimes prayer is a spontaneous hallelujah.

I know a woman whose husband suffered for years from a debilitating disease. In an especially difficult turn for the worse, he was admitted to the hospital. This time, however, it was different, because this time, it really seemed like the end. The doctors confirmed that her husband lay dying. It will be any time now, they said. A week passed. Any minute now. Days passed. The waiting was so hard. The man lay in bed, curled up, unresponsive. For days there was no discernible pulse, six to eight breaths a minute. Any second now. Two days passed. Three days. And then, suddenly, it stopped. Silence.

"It's over," she said when I answered the phone.

"Just like the morning rain," I thought.

At his grave, we said *Kaddish*; in Jewish tradition, the ancient prayer for the mourner, the prayer of all prayers. *Kaddish* is the exclamation point to our sorrow and loss, because its words contain the declaration that despite all our tragedies, despite our pain and suffering, we affirm that life is good, we affirm holiness, and we praise the God of grandeur. And to that we say "amen" over and over again.

And so, I have begun to understand a bit. Life at its core is a mystery, much of it ultimately unknowable—why people live, why people die, why the rains cause floods or suddenly stop for months, causing drought. Why there is suffering. It is all, I realize, so unknowable. In fact, years ago, in the aftermath of September 11, 2001, I declared that I finally understood spiritual principle number one, the principle that drives it all. Spiritual principle number one is: I know nothing. And only in this perpetual state of not knowing can my heart begin to open in prayer.

And maybe, just maybe, prayer and "amen" are the same—a gentle yet steady embrace of the mystery.

Prayer is an articulation of our highest desires, our yearnings, our dark places, a reflection of the light we hold within. It is a conversation with the invisible, an acknowledgment of the mystery, a query into the ineffable. When we pray, we reach for clarity, for strength beyond what we know. Praying is at once an intense self-examination and a dialogue with the sacred, representing the seam of a very fine fabric where the physical is joined to the metaphysical, and where, no matter our reason for praying, we touch a bit of heaven.

Prayer has been my tether, my sandbox, my joy. And amen is the punctuation to the perpetual search.

This is my offering.

Section I
Awakening the Spiritual Path

Bearing Witness

Every day that we are gifted
another moment of life,
we are offered an invitation
to awaken the spirit to
the grandeur and reality of love.

We are summoned
to bear witness to the beauty
and miracle of everyday living.

To bear witness
 is the crucial step
toward becoming fully human.

Beholden

O God of the Lunar Light
reflect Your mercies upon me.
Cast my gaze upon the many miracles,
the joy sustained,
the hallelujah of the
midnight
sky.

My slumbering soul is unaware.
I walk in beauty, made lovely
by a billion nightlights,
surrounded by blessings
and grace.

How have I become unnoticing?
What great pain has rendered me
unaware, dazed?

Lift me, shake me, toss me out into the wonder.
I am so small, so gratefully small.

You are the context. I am beholden.

Teach me to exclaim, to proclaim, to abide the quiet
and embrace the grandeur faithfully.
To say and shout and sing
Your holy praises.
Hallelujah.

Tumble Prayer

Make your prayer tumble
like sagebrush driven by the wind,
any wind, here and there
circling with dirt and dust
down a quiet road.

Everything else abandoned.
Apparent randomness,
no matter, no thought, no purpose
other than to be taken. A surrender of reason.
Tumble, stumble, thorny prayer

driven by breeze, breath, and sigh,
gathering the nitty-gritty as it grabs
whatever is offered up upon the dry
hot lands of open space.

Open to the winds,
open to the ground,
open to the air.
Open to the rumble of journey.
Open to the real understanding
that we roll along pretending to be
masters of all, and we are not.

And that is prayer.

Submit the heart and the will
to supplication and hope and optimism,
that we may bear this journey with joy,
tumbled and thorny as it may be.

Only This

I ask of You,
O God,
only this.

Grant me:
a curious mind,
an agitated conscience,
an open and discerning heart,
a surrendering spirit.

And then,

and then,

I shall become a
servant of the holy good.

God of Mercy

O God of mercy,
I offer the core of my being,
my open heart.
I cast my gaze downward.
Palms turn upward in supplication,
and generosity, and love.

It is good to walk gently
with the breath of mortality
upon my cheek.
It humanizes.

O God of life and death,
I walk in humility before
all that is good and lovely and loving
and oh so temporary.

All Is Possible

Discern,
oh heart of mine,
the drops of mist
upon the grass,
in the early light,
glistening
with possibility.

All is possible.

Delight me
with the
nourishing mystery
of Presence.

Then will my heart
rejoice and I
will take my place
amid the Glory
of Your creation.

I Wake Before the Dawn

Before the rising of the sun,
streams of light escape,
radiating upon the early morning
sky, still dim from the night.

This is what I need to learn.

I pledge to wake
before the dawn
and sit quietly in the darkness,
no noise but the house
that shifts and moans.
No sound but the avenue
of cars on their way.
No motion but a cup of coffee,
and maybe a book of poems
or a volume of luminous thoughts
and the votive upon my desk,
and breath.

Anticipation, really,
that as the light bursts forth
and morning prevails
I may learn,
through the sheer repetition of
of the rising sun upon
the horizon, clouded or clear,
that really
light cannot be contained.
Incapable, actually.

Call Upon Me

Dear God,
Ruler of all things,
of destiny,
of human endeavor,
guide me
that I may serve You
and be in service to
the highest good.

Call upon me,
pursue me,
I am here.

Waiting

Hold the pose, my teacher said,

breathing in breathing out
breathing in breathing out

pushing against the resistance.

Sometimes,
waiting is knowing.

Sometimes
you have to live a little longer
to understand.

It is called unfolding.

The pause,
the long inhale
and exhale of living.
The waiting.

Push gently
against the edge,
that sacred place,
that thin ethereal fragile line
between can and can't
where God touches us
with possibility.

breathing in breathing out
breathing in breathing out

holding,
Held.

Resilience

A voice calls out
in the darkest part of my night.
An unfamiliar sound.
A question.

I wonder,
what is the difference between those who are
defeated by their life's circumstance
and those who are not?

And then suddenly, revelation. A defining moment.
An unexpected defiance.

I shake my fist at the heavens and declare with strength and
power and determination
you're not going to get me. You are not going to get me.

And the monster shudders,
just a bit.
And the shadows pull back,
just a bit.
And the despair weakens,
just a bit.
And I know that from this moment there is no turning back.

This pain will not defeat me.

The Archaeologist of the Soul

I suppose that the archaeologist
delights in brokenness.
Shards are proof of life.
Though a vessel, whole, but dusty
and rare, is also good.

I suppose that the archaeologist
does not agonize over the charred
lines of destruction signifying
a war, a conquest, a loss, a fire,
or a complete collapse.
The blackened layer
seared upon the balk
is discovery.

So why do I mourn,
and shiver,
and resist?
Why do I weep
as I dig deeper
and deeper still?
Dust, dirt,
buckets of rubble,
brokenness,
a fire or two,
shattered layers
of a life that
rebuilds upon
the discarded,
the destroyed,
and then
the reconstructed,

only to break again,
and deeper still,
shards upon shards,
layers upon layers.

If you look carefully,
the earth reveals its secrets.
So does the soul,
and the cell,
and the sinew,
and the thought,
and the wisp of memory,
and the laugh,
and the cry,
and the heart,
that seeks its deepest truth,
digging down,
down to bedrock.

Rock bottom they call it,
and in Hebrew,
the Mother Rock.

God of grace,
teach me
that the layers
of brokenness
create a whole.

Whispers

God speaks in whispers.
Silent brushes of wind,
moments that
implore you to take notice.

There is so much that I do not understand:
How to sing when I am choking.
How to forget.
How to remember.
How to discern the blessing within the pain.
How to heal so that I may
hold on to greatness and grandeur.

Rather,
I wish for softness and stillness,
for the relinquishment of all that no longer matters.
I wish for goodness to linger like the scent of jasmine
on a hot summer day.
It's enough already. It's enough
resenting people and circumstances so far away
that even the scars have dulled with age.

Out there, beyond my small self,
is vastness and forgiveness and fortitude and love.
I long to fall gently into the arms of a loving world.

God speaks in whispers
silent brushes of wind and
moments that implore you to take notice.

At Some Point We Wake

At some point,
we wake to the reality of our mortality.
At some moment,
the veil of illusion is pulled back and
we see the angel of death peering
from the heart of mystery.
At first, we are frightened, even terrified.

And then,
if grace be upon us,
life comes into sharper focus,
and we sort out the trivial
from the vital.
And fear is supplanted by gratitude.

Humility

A yielding at the center.
Presence without want.
Cast your eyes downward,
the ground beneath your feet is holy.

Lift Me
A Morning Song

I lay my doubts upon the land like the mist of early
morning.
A fallen cloud has left a sheen upon the field,
upon my fearful heart.

Enter the mysteries of my emerging self.
Lift the weight from my aching heart
like the rising sun dispels the damp traces
of the fallen clouds of early morning.

I offer myself, my doubt, my insecurities, my fear.
I am so afraid. I wait to be taken.

Lift me, God. I call this grace.

Holy One of clarity, take me
and I shall rise.

Quiet My Soul, O Holy One

Still the sounds that torment my mind
and make my heart weep.
At times the quiet is deafening
and the silences lonely,
I pray and I wait.
The difference,
dear God,
is You.
Gently still my fears
so that my heart
may hear and rejoice
and peace may descend
like a steady rain at daybreak.

Quiet my soul, O Holy One.
Still the sounds that torment my mind
and enter my silences with an inner stirring,
for love is in the quiet of God's presence
and I long to surrender into the hush.

Trust

It's called Diving into the Wreck,[1]
I told her.
These are the healing years,
I told her.
You are so brave.
I know it's frightening, but once
you clean out a bit of the darkness,
your heart will begin to open and
light will emerge,
I told her.
Be brave.
And just think about it,
I said.
We are all wreckage waiting to be found.
And in the wreckage,
treasure.

Meaning

And Elijah stood upon rock,
in the cleft of the cave.
And God passed by.
What are you doing here, Elijah?

What are you doing here?

Learning

All that has happened teaches and enlightens.
Each and every learning
is a choice, a decision on how to proceed.

Let no hurt distract your path from good,
nor pain divert your intention from love.

Learn the divine purpose for your life
and live there.

Decide

Today I decide
to turn my eyes toward wonder,
so that I may see the expanse before me.

Today I decide to see the possibility of my life,
so that I may open my mind to greatness.

Today I will do one kindness,
so that my heart may become more loving.

Today I will pause to consider,
so that my life may become more deliberate.

Help me, dear God, to step
firmly upon a path of consequence,
so that I may make my life a prayer
of goodness and mercy, splendor and light.

I ask for a life of meaning,
a sense of purpose.
Today I decide.

Always Mortal

Moments before the lightning hit the engine of the plane
I fell asleep. The kind of lull of consciousness
that makes the chin drop low into the chest.
What woke me was the sensation of a child's hand
upon my shoulder, an angel's breath upon my cheek.
I looked up, then out the window, a lightning strike,
a flash of light, a sharp thump, a pop.
All in one quick moment.
OK then, I said, aloud,
with no one to hear,
and with no fear.
None.

I have nothing more to say about this except
that I have felt the hand of an angel before,
and honestly, were it not for the updraft
of some divine thing, I would not be here now.
More than once. More than twice.
Many more times than that.

You don't have to be reckless
to need the help of angels, though I was.
You just need to fly into the storm with faith,
the belief that the pilot will know what to do.
And I am rather sure that the pilot has also felt
the small wise hand of fate
and called it angel,
an imagined touch
that leaves its imprint
upon the soul.

In truth,
I will never forget the day
that I understood I am always at risk.

Always.

Always mortal.
On a plane, in a war zone, in bed,
in the car on the way to the pharmacy,
standing in line to pick up tickets,
crossing the street after a few too many glasses of wine, or
just crossing at the crosswalk, after the light changes green
and the oncoming car doesn't stop. Sitting on the couch watching
silly television shows. Stirring the sugar and almond milk
in a morning cup of coffee. Lighting a scented candle
against the dark cold night.

Always mortal.
The last breath
taken
suddenly,
or slowly,
aware,
unaware,
always
mortal.

And so I call upon the angels.
I want to go without fear.
And in the meantime,
and this is most important,

I want to live without fear.

Is that one wish or two?
O Angel of God,
how many wishes do I have?

Fear and Hope

Inside the human heart is fear.
There is also hope.
The two wrestle constantly, like Jacob and his God.
Sometimes one prevails. Sometimes the other.
The struggle is sometimes silent, other times loud.
But it is constant—fear, hope, fear, hope.
Flashes of light and shadow twirling inside us all the time.

It is so much easier when there is love.
When love is in your life
it becomes the context for it all.
Love is the measure of a life well lived,
it is the beacon of possibility.
When you love, the fear is less harsh,
hope a bit stronger.

Presence

God who brings forth light and distinction.
Teach me a secret or two.

Forever noticing, sorting, sifting, discerning, examining.
Detail sanctifies the mundane.

Attention is a creative act.

I, who is created in Your image, am compelled to
announce, to proclaim:

The brown wave, turning and churning the sand that has
traveled the journey
of thousands of miles.

The last iris hiding in limestone in the Gilboa Mountains,
blackish purple,
alive but for a moment.

The wine stain left last night by the bottle's bottom,
careless red,
flushed conversation.

The muddy eyes of the infant son, unfocused, crossed,
wandering,
brilliant.

The cane supporting a prophet of mortality whose
translucent hands,
clenched, hold on to another day.

O God, call upon my presence,
that I may be a helping hand to holiness.

Supplication

Some mornings are cement gray.
It may merely be the predawn hour,
or maybe the heavy clouds that fell to earth.
It may be that my heart is filled with sadness,
or eyes hazy, a disconcerting development,
so much out of focus.

Some mornings arrive with acute ambiguity.
All days begin unsure. Every day a dilemma.
To notice or ignore. To touch or immerse.
To skate and skim, or play, or lie, or to
dive deeply into meaning, foggy as it may be,
and if so, pray, pray into the haze.

Supplication.

I am begging for my life.
I'm begging You, O Wonder of the universe.
I bow before the greatest power of all.
To You, the vague and hazy mystery.
To You, the context for all questions,
encompassing all confusion.

I bow before You.

Where is the secret hiding place of Jacob's angels?
Reveal yourself, I implore.
Come forth from the fog.
And I, I bow before the obscure.
Knees touching the earth.
Toes touching the earth.
Palms touching the earth.
Forehead touching the earth.

Home of the worm,
origin of the mother and father,
home of the grave,
pillow to my head.

Supplication.

Repentance

Repentance,
a turning,
a returning,
to the path that
leads you to your highest good.

The Creative Spirit

From the first burst of light,
from the root of all being,
from the source of all that is good,
from the moment the human was born,
we were gifted with a creative spirit.

Learning to Yield

B'rachah,
a gentle bending,
bowing,
humbling of self-
centeredness.

To ask of God is a blessing,
a blessing to place divinity at the core of your being. For
this,
bending works best.

Dear God,
I long for Your blessing.
Help me turn aside my pain, fear,
doubt
so that I may be filled with the
light of Your goodness.

My God,
I reach out for Your staff
to guide and comfort me.
Lead me to a stillness of soul,
so that my life may become
blessing.

And I know
that there are those who bend because they are
doubled over in pain.
Touch my fingers with kindness, dear One,
that I may wipe their tears with holiness.
Sweet God,
I bow my head in reverence,
yearning to be free of

the silliness that makes me stumble,
the trembling that makes me falter, and
the voices that take me off course.

B'rachah,
a gentle bending
bowing
humbling of self-
centeredness.
Oh, that I may be filled with the
light of Your goodness.

Stretch Out Your Light

Oh encrusted heart of mine,
I implore you: let go.
Let go of all that was
and then receive in humility
the presence of your inherent greatness.
And then, let go of that as well.

Stretch out your light
like the arms of a child anticipating
an embrace from her father,
returning home.

Returning home, I say.
Returning home.

Loss Is a Cleansing

I was on my way,
quite unaware
of the burden
upon my soul
and my gripping heart
clenching what was,
and I heard,
a sound from
a distance place,
from my inner being
saying,

Loss is a
cleansing.
Don't hold on,
let it fall away,
you can't hold on,
no anger will soothe,
no regret will restore,
let it go, for what is lost,
is simply gone.
And I answered,
Slow my breath,
Holy One,
that I may receive
Your abundant
gifts.

Love

Whatever the question,
love
is
the
answer.

And often
gratitude.

And always
love.

Turn to the Light

Hope is the opposite of
cynicism.

Say,
Despite what is probable,
all is possible.

Say,
We are only limited
by our imagination.

Say,
The universe abundantly
provides.

Be
like the sunflower,
scan the heavens for the light.

Turn toward the light.

Resolve

Collect yourself.
Anger. Hurt. Guilt.
You have given so much away.

Gather what you can,
for you have scattered
the only power that you have.

This is the great resolve—
a reclamation of power.
We must not be ruled by fear,
or revenge, or insult, or pain.

There is loveliness upon your heart,
let that be your guide.

To the God of Enigma

I understand paradox.
I really do.

Memory is alive.

Exposed, down to the bark,
the tree is so real,
essential,
without
distraction.
It just is.

And look!
The silver bark of a tree
having lost its leaves, is a glistening sheen.

You may have lost all hope because the leaves,
with so much beauty,
have betrayed their
loveliness and
fallen
to the muddled ground
and left you bare
and cold and
exposed.

But the stripped-down tree is
about hope.
It is like a sculpture,
alive with light and strength,
majestically arching its branches
here and there, reaching,
like the arms of the ballerinas

who have practiced their pose
to delight and awe.

Because the tree remembers that it is connected
to the mind of the Ancient One, it knows a singular truth:

All will change.
And change again.

And the starkness will disappear behind the buds
and then the bloom, and then the leaves and then the fall.
And memory is alive.

Light and Dust

God of light and dust
I am so very lonely.

So much depends upon me
to be right, to be wise, to fix,
to make it happen, to lead,
in control,
all-knowing,
all-powerful,

I am exhausted.

Dear God,
place me as a speck upon a ray of light,
illuminated like a particle of dust
in the sweep of destiny.

I reach my hand across the expanse,
I turn to You in prayerful discernment
and walk as a faithful partner,
doing what I can,
what I must,
what is in my power,
no more, no less,
constant and sure,
and then, letting go of the rest.
Letting go. Let it be.

O God of all,
Source and Sustainer of mystery,
teach me, guide me, open my heart,
that I may live with renewed energy,
and humility and limited consequence.

Choosing

There is a moment in time when
you see a flash of light, or feel a slight wisp of wind,
or notice a momentary pause
as if the world is holding its breath.

And then suddenly, at that moment,
your life comes into focus.
And it is that very moment
that beckons you to take a turn in the road
and step on a path
that leads you to the truth of who you are.

And in the moment, in the light,
in the whisper of wind, in the pause,
you have a choice that can change your life forever.
You can choose to live.
To *really* live,
or to simply get along.

Choose to live.

Atonement

I have been a hand glider,
a digger of desert wells,
a tramp and an addict.
But mostly I've come up empty.

My heart is buried and distant
and oddly focused elsewhere,
a never-never land of wilderness
and barren landscape bereft of meaning,
of love, of belonging,
of longing for anything real.
How did this place become my home?
I am lost. I am lost. I am gone.

Break the shackles, the binding
of a sad and empty heart.
Free me from past afflictions.
Banish the stupor from my numb and
crackling soul that insists
I reach for dust day after day.
I am a prisoner to emptiness,
held captive by invisible fears and unspoken
terror long ago muted, silenced by substance
and static and the melody of a self-made demon.

Speak to me of story, Invisible God,
of return, of home, of soul, of pain,
of a life before the unsteady balance.
Teach me to touch again, to be touched,
to feel.
I want
my days,

my days,
my days,
a simple day.

Help me, Healer of the wounds,
demand of me atonement, lest my
introspection become another selfish indulgence.
Cast me out, send me forth and then
catch my soaring spirit, lightly snaring me
in the net of a better day.

Hold me, keep me, protect me.

Hope Is the Bridge

The psalmist cries:
O God of all being, my God
I have cried out to You
And You have healed me.
Weeping may linger in the night
But at dawn there is joy. (Psalm 30:3, 30:6)

Hope is the bridge
To the next stage of your life.
Go forward.
With hope in your heart,
You will not fall.

Hold Me in Prayer

My heart is broken.
The weight of it all bears down upon me,
I am bent over, crumbling, and diminished.
And through my tears, my confusion,
I have a thought, a glimmer,
or maybe
an invitation from the Invisible One.

If my heart is already broken, cracked open,
why not spend some time looking inside?

And so, I offer this prayer:

This most difficult and vulnerable moment,
this moment of sorrow and pain and uncertainty
has opened my heart.

Before the healing,
help me linger,
exposed,
aware,
unafraid,
willing
to understand my heart,
my soul,
my fears,
my brokenness,
my depth,
myself.
Expansive God,
hold me, hear my prayer.

The Ghost of Love

This morning I sat alone, perfectly still in the darkness of an empty sanctuary void of worshipers, of prayer, of music. I listened to the silence, trying to hear the prayers of the many souls that had been there. I wondered, what do they pray when no one is listening? Then, I heard a faint echo. It was like the sound of lives in wonder: a choir of sighs and song, of high and low notes, of harmony and dissonance. And in the darkness of the empty sanctuary, I was comforted. I realized that life is not about one painful moment in time. Rather, it is an arc of time. And in that arc, countless souls have prayed and found some small measure of wonder. And despite all the pain, in that small measure of wonder, a light bursts forth.

And in the light—forgiveness.

Overflow
The Prayer of the Well Digger

I did not notice
the dawn.
All possibility eluded me.
So immersed was I
in the dull and numbing
routine of a driving force
to succeed, to accomplish,
a restlessness, a compulsion.
Vanity. Emptiness.

And then, with compassion
and without judgment
a gentle engagement
tugged me out of my
complacency

and behold.
Behold the breath

and the dawn returns
and the emptiness
has meaning
like a well,
hewn by nature
by God
by the
will to
Overflow
and I
draw upon
the waters

of Eden
nourished by the
Source of all good
and instead of an
ordinary day,
extraordinary,
endlessly filled
with possibility.

This the prayer
of the well digger.

Guide Me

Dearest God,
Creator of light,
You set before me
blessing, life, goodness.

Guide me, comfort me.

Through my longing,
gently urge me to find my life's purpose.

Like the grasses of the field
bend to the wind
I bow, humble.
I choose life.

Hide and Seek

All my life I have played hide and seek.

Hide.
Seek.

Hiding from You, dear One.
And from myself, from my faults,
from the dusty parts of my soul
that have not seen light in so many years,
that are afraid to face what needs to be seen
what needs to emerge, what needs repair.

Expose me, O God.
I search for Your presence
for the courage, for the strength
to become known, to be found,
and to smooth out the rough spots,
and to live, and to be fearless
in the truth of who I am
and what I can offer and
who I can become
and not to
hide.

Find me.

Return

With great impatience,
and pain and yearning,
the world awaits
redemption.

As do I.

Splintered from the Source
I seek wholeness
and return.

Abundance

Two perspectives govern our way
of seeing the world: abundance and scarcity.
These perspectives are a choice.

The cup is not half empty,
nor is it half full.
Rather our cup runneth over,
overflowing.

My Rock

God,
like stones in the river,
carry me across.
You are my Rock
and my Redeemer.

Give Away the Pain

Forgiveness is not an emotion
that erases all wounds.
We cannot condone.
We do not forget.
We release the anger and pain.
When we for*give*,
we *give* away the pain that binds us.

Perpetual Crossings

I walk softly on the damp wooded path.
Mostly I look down
and see the ground beneath my feet is
soft earth, gentle moss,
and, of course, fallen leaves, which,
like angels, have floated to earth
forming a gently lit path in the woods.

And for every chasm along the way,
for every fast-moving stream or deeply cut valley,
a bridge appears.
It seems that there is always
a way across,
a way to get to the other side of fear, of sadness, of
disappointment.
There is always a way.

Maybe goodness is the bridge, or beauty is the bridge.
Love is the bridge.
Forgiveness is the bridge.

Of this I am sure:
the path is eternal—it is our life and the length of our days.

And the bridge is eternal—
there are many ways to cross what seems impossible.
Stones in the river, ropes suspended, planks of wood,
arches of steel like love, patience, acceptance
and forgiveness.

A Simple Awareness

Sometimes I think that God's love
is a simple moment of awareness,
a knowing that lives deep within,
a sensation, a whisper, an understanding
that I am not alone.

And the only thing I must do
is not deny, or ignore, but rather,
implore,

God,
help me live in the sweep of some great
love.

Doubt

Take your well-held beliefs
and put them aside.

Despite what we are taught,
there are many ways,
many paths,
many options.

You are only limited by your imagination.

Do not doubt your heart.

Courage

And I said:
O if only I had wings like the dove
I would fly away and find a restful abode.
I would wander afar while hastening
to find a haven from the stormy tempest. (Psalm 55:7–9)

And so I pray
that my spirit have the strength to soar,
that my heart have the courage to seek,
and my mind the wisdom to discover,
a life of meaning and purpose.

Grant me, O God,
strength,
courage,
and wisdom.

Build a Vessel of Compassion

We are all broken,
working out the dents.
We are tender beings.
The fragments have sharp edges and carry sparks of light.
This is the truth of our humanity:
To take what is shattered, piece by piece,
 and build a vessel of beauty, of compassion.

God of All Things

Sometimes we see the world
as if it falls short of what we need.
There is never enough, there is always something missing.
The foundation is somehow cracked, leaking goodness.
When we believe this, we are afraid.

When we are afraid, we behave badly.

Sometimes we see the world
as if it is filled with possibility.
There is a consistent sense of hope, there is always a way.
The foundation on which we stand is firm, opportunity
abounds.
When we believe this, we foster inner peace.

When we are at peace, we are more loving.

Each way of seeing the world
is a perspective on life, and a choice.
We choose to see a world of scarcity.
We choose to see a world of abundance.

God of all things,
May I choose to live abundantly.
And then choose again.
And again.

Life Defined

If you stay angry forever
the one who has wronged you will win.
If you hold on to your anger
as self-defense or
as self-protection,
eventually you will lose
because the pain of that anger will begin
to define you.

Love life.
And allow the loving presence
of the Spirit of the universe to
live in your core.
Love life.
And its wonders and miracles
will give you renewed purpose for living.

Open My Eyes

To gaze and
to linger.
To cultivate
the practice of pause.

This is the revolution!

To liberate the light
from the dull and routine
way we walk through this life.

How would you be in this world,
what would you say
if you somehow understood
that your true purpose is
to be a testifying witness?

Discern

The Dove of Silence, I prayed:

Be gracious unto me
for I am surrounded by people who wish to consume me.

And then came the day when I was most afraid
and I put my trust in You.

When I surrender to faith,
fear steps aside and I fall silent.

What power do others truly have over my spirit?

Peace is like a dove, gracefully soaring,
silent, humble in beauty.

Help understand my path, to heed the callings
of my greatest potential.

To the Morning God

This morning,
I was awakened by the sound of prayer.
It was not a prayer like most.
I did not hear
dear God or
blessed are You or
King of the universe,
or even
Holy One full of compassion.

Rather, it began with the noise
that rain makes
when it shatters the silence of night.

At first it was light and steady,
gentle, yet unrelenting,
and then suddenly burst forth
and pounded the earth.
As I listened to its rage
and watched it fill the windowsill
and glisten with darkness,
I thought, this is the sound of
heaven meeting earth.

Forgiveness

Forgiveness is a process, a path without an end,
a bridge that leads to restoration
of what you have lost.

It is a shift of perspective,
a way of being.

Forgiveness is what you do to your soul when you
choose to live in light rather than in darkness.

A More Gentle Voice

I call across the canyon
to my inner being.
Are you there?
Are you there?
And an echo returns:
You are small.
You are small.
And then,
you are not enough,
and enough.

And so it goes.
Years of struggle,
back and forth, to and fro.
I am small, not enough.

I have nurtured
the critic, the judge,
the negative inner voice
long enough.

Oh lovely one,
are you there?

God of affirmation,
God of love,
God of beauty,
God of emptiness,
God of space.
I call upon a more loving,
gentle and forgiving
force that has always lived
quietly, silently within.

I call upon You.
and a quiet radical voice
rising,
rising
above the abyss.

I am here.
I am here.
I am here.

I am my beloved's,
And my beloved is mine.

The Truth

The only regrets I have in my life
are the times when I was ungracious.
When my limitations diminished my capacity for love.
When I was so small and filled with self
that my need to be right blinded me to the largeness of
the truth.

This is the truth:
Life is short. Often tragic. At times, joyful.
Forgive yourself for all those times when you forgot,
or didn't know, or didn't understand, or ignored,
or didn't have the inner strength to live
this truth.

Hope, Banish My Despair

Creator of darkness and light,
banish my despair,
turn aside my indifference,
soften the callousness of my heart.

Open my eyes
that I may see that
beauty abounds
and love abides.

Enlighten my life with
holiness and grace.
As it is written:
Come, let us walk in the light of God. (Isaiah 2:5)

A Nighttime Prayer

Fear not
as the night takes hold.
Lay down your head
and be assured that
there are no dragons here
where brave souls
confront and battle
and defy
and then cradle
the frightened
ghosts that linger
and linger
and stay.

This is your moment.
Become the hero of your life,
for heroes are made in battle,
and the courageous triumph,
knowing when to fight
and when to reconcile.

We do not banish what pursues us.
We take dictation.
We are faithful students of
the broken heart,
learning what needs
to be learned,
and letting go of the rest.

Cradle the frightened ghosts
that linger in the night.
They have taught

you compassion,
and are no match
for your love.

God of the broken heart,
hear our nighttime prayer.

Presence

And all that we really have,
and all that we can really give,
is presence.

Just to be
present.

To the God of Another Day
A Song

I've been summoned by the
white light of day.
The sky a flat grey veil.
An ordinary day,
bright and barely noticeable
in its usual garb.

And then, suddenly,
the morning light
is golden
upon the wall.
Splashes
against
all things,
radiating
along the objects
of my daily life.

And the corner
of my lonely room
becomes
alive,
and a bright light
of defiance glimmers
upon the wall
like a wave
of beauty
to banish
the shadows.

Blessings upon another day.
Blessings upon today.

Linger

Stay a while,
O fickle thought, that I may

Practice sacred.
Practice elevated thought.
Practice sustained thought.
Practice stillness.
Practice non-thought.

Help me, O Holy One of silence,
to cultivate a gentle way of being in the world.
Reveal Your truth and beauty that they
may be at the core of my desire.

May I learn to liberate the light
from the dull and routine way
in which I see the world.
Help me to regard, not merely to see,
to linger, not merely to walk.

To breathe.
To consider.
And to speak.
May my very being
beautify this world.

Wonder

Embrace the world with wonder.
Less judgment,
more amazement.

In Between

How I long for twilight.
The very moment of in
between.
The dance
between sun and moon,
daily,
generating light,
reflecting light.

And, I too,
daily radiating light,
reflecting light.

I scan the heavens.
I wait to witness when both are visible.
The two great lights,
one of day and one of night,
both of heaven and earth,
one rising, the other disappearing.

Rising.
Setting.
Still.
Not here.
Not there.
And yet, where?
Where did you go?

God of ambiguity,
I ask You,
You know my heart,
Have I always lived in some perpetual twilight?

In between.

Where are You?
Are You in the in
between?

To the Uplifting God
Help Me

I.
The longer I live,
the more I understand that
the power is in the question.
Not the answer.

Questions launch me,
set me on a quest,
they propel.
Answers provide a bench along the path,
a stationary place to rest.
Who wouldn't want an answer?

And yet, I feel more alive
in the quest, in the movement,
even in the uncertainty.
When I am sure, I feel small.

II.
Take my outstretched hand,
pull me through the
wondrous mystery of living.
Raise me up upon
a path in the wilderness.
For I long to be
servant to the mystery,
friend to largeness of thought,
steward of the question.

Help me be a vagabond wandering
through Your boundless world.

May astonishment be my guide.
I stand before You
curious, unknowing, willing
to live in ambiguity.
Steady me as I ask

what is the great question of my life,
the propelling force?

I wonder
more than I know.

Ordinary Splendor

Its the ordinary light
that got to me today.

Brightness
despite the clouds,

clarity
despite the opaque white sky.

We live for these moments.
For the ease of discernment

that all is well, or good enough,
and actually, quite spectacular.

Simply grand
because what is,
simply is.

Another day.
And behold,
I awoke to declare
its splendor.

Amen

God, enduring Mystery of life,
I have heard the call to awakening.
Rouse me from an unconscious slumber.

Make my prayer a wordless embrace
of all I cannot understand
and allow my heart
to acknowledge the wonder in life,
even in the midst of struggle.

Dear God,
for the mystery
and for the silence,
teach me to say
amen.

Imagination

Within me a well, deep, filled with cool abundant water.

God,
sweet muse of love and loveliness!
Turn my thoughts toward You
that my eyes may see
and my heart may know
and my mind may remember
that there is beauty in my dreams.

Beyond me, a vision, a clear yet winding way.

Invisible God, eternal God,
God of holiness and wonder,
awaken my spirit so that
I may envision
and behold
and make real
a universe of light.

In the palm of my hand, all things possible.

Make of Me a Vessel

I call upon the deep, the dark,
the hovering spirit, the God of creation,
the muse of the creative impulse.

Make of me a vessel,
ready to receive
the loving stream from
a transcendent good,
that it may course its way
through my discerning mind
and complicated heart
and the purity of my soul,
O aspirational soul,
so that I may be
a force for good.

For in the beginning it was very good.

And this is our human destiny.
To be created in the image of those earliest moments of
divinity—

when the darkness danced
in flowing circles with light
and beauty cast a hue
upon all things
simple and complex,
known and unknown,
returning,
always turning toward
the deep dark
hovering spirit of

the God
of creation.

I call upon You,
Creator of the universe,
make of me a vessel, a mere image
of paradoxical beauty.
Of mystery.
And oneness.
And love.

And love.

To the God of Simple Elegance
Hallelujah

I don't know Your name
but I know the translucent petals
pushing against the air
with violet wonder,
cradled by green leaves, sunlit,
quivering in the wind.

How majestic is the work of creation.
Wisdom and simplicity.
This is our greatest inheritance.
A most joyful love.

Gratitude

Imagine how your life would change
if you awoke every morning and declared:
Thank You, God, for Your abundant gifts.

And imagine if things weren't going so well
and still you awoke every morning
and said: Thank You, God, for Your abundant gifts.

How would that change your life?

Release Me

May it be Your will,
Divine Source of truth,
that a grateful disposition
be my way.

Prevail upon me.
Rid me
of obstacle.
I am stubborn,
holding on,
obstinate,
set in my ways.

Release me.
Release the ghosts of the past

to contentment
and gratitude.

Joy

I believe in the night.
I await those rare times
when my heart spills its weight
like the Big Dipper into darkness.

This is faith.
What is seen is velvet black
and quiet and still,
and yes.

And then, for a moment,
until the dawn impatiently
shakes off the silence,
the night reveals its secrets.

The joy of predawn.

SECTION II
God's Tears

GRIEF AND MOURNING

Dying
To the God, Who Teaches

Do not fear the moment
when the border is near like the blue line,
thin upon the horizon.

Do not fear.

Dying is not a fearful thing.
Release the dread
like a child releases a helium balloon,
red, rising, toward the heavens,
the boundary between known and not known.

You cannot control this moment.
Not any of it.
Let go of the fear.

Rather, climb upon the seesaw,
and pray that the rocking
back and forth, back and forth,
be gentle, be kind.
One side, the weight of sadness,
the other the lift of love.
Love, sadness, love, sadness, sadness, love.
Back and forth, a gentle rocking
like it was, back in the womb.

And then,
the world contracts, becomes small.
Fewer visits, less talking, the bed envelops
the body that seems to disappear, sinking back
into the womb of preexistence.
Just breath, barely breath.

Swaying, sadness, love, sadness, love.

And the blue line nears,
the boundary emerges, envelops.
And all is peace.
No fear, only love.
Only love, a canopy of peace.

And then,
no longer a border, no longer the boundary,
but a hue between
now and eternity.

God, guard my parting and my return,
now and forever.
Amen. Selah.

I Lift My Eyes
Esa Einai

I am searching for words
For the words that describe,
Make sense, or at least comfort.
Words that summon me from the depths
Of my solitude.

In the night, there is darkness.
Restless attempts to sleep,
Twisting, turning into the shadows.
As I seek a comfortable pose
I bring my knees to my chest
Folding my dreams in half;
Will the crease ever come out?

And in the day there are
Silent attempts to find hope.
Twisting, turning toward the light
As I look for direction, a path, a way.

It is not easy to find the way.
And so,
I lift my eyes to the mountains.
Heaven lays her head upon the mountaintop
And I begin to climb.

What is the source of my help?
I climb and gaze upon the vistas.
More mountains, more horizons
Never-ending moments where heaven meets earth,
Never-ending possibilities to meet the Divine.

Lift me, carry me, offer me courage.
Help me understand life's sharpest paradox:
That to live is tragic and wonderful,
Painful and awesome, dark and filled with light.

I lift my eyes to the summit
And as I climb I find my help
In the turning and twisting it takes to
Ascend.
I have found a path and it is worn and charted
By all those who are summoned from solitude.
I take their lead.
And I know that in the most essential way
I am being carried up the mountain.
And even now,
Dear God, even now
I am not alone.

Learning from Death

The true worth of a life
Is the story it has left behind.
Tell it well.
Search for meaning and understanding.
Search for the truth:
Did he teach you about love?
Did she personify genius or sensitivity?
Did his life warn you of the danger of bitterness and anger?

As I stand and behold the eyes
Of those who mourn, I realize
That the only difference between people in this world
Is not their wealth, fame, or success.
The only difference is
Those who had love in their life
And those who did not.

From a Mother to Her Girls

The morning you wake to bury me
you'll wonder what to wear.
The sun may be shining, or maybe it will rain.
It may be winter. Or not.
You'll say to yourself, black, aren't you supposed to
wear black? Then you will remember all the times we went
together to buy clothes: the prom, homecoming,
just another pair of jeans,
another sweater, another pair of shoes. I called you my
Barbie dolls.
You will remember how I loved to dress you.
How beautiful you were in my eyes.

The morning you wake to bury me
you will look in the mirror in disbelief.
You'll reach for some makeup. Or not. And you won't
believe that
this is the morning you will bury your mother.
But it is. And as you gaze into that mirror, you will
shed a tear. Or not. But look. Look carefully,
for hiding in your expression, you will find mine.
You will see me in your eyes, in the way you laugh.
You will feel me when you think of God,
and of love and struggle.

Look into the mirror and you will see me in a look, or in
the way you hold your mouth or stand, a little bent, or
maybe straight.
But you will see me.

So let me tell you, one last time, before you dress,
what to wear. Put on any old thing. Black or red, skirt or pants.

Despite what I told you all these years, it doesn't really matter.
Because as I told you all these years, you are beautiful the way you are.
Dress yourself in honor and dignity.
Dress yourself in confidence and self-love.
Wear a sense of obligation for this world,
for you are one of the lucky ones and there is so much to do, to fix.
Take care of each other,
take care of your heart, of your soul.
Talk to God.
Wear humility and compassion.

When you wake to bury me,
put on a strong sense of self, courage, and understanding.
I am sorry. Forgive me. I am sorry.
Stand at my grave clothed in a gown of forgiveness,
dressed like an angel would be, showing compassion
and unconditional love.
For at that very moment, all that will be left of me to give is love.
Love.

For My Father

After my father died,

a blanket fell upon my heart.
You know, that gentle way a parent
pulls the covers around your small body,
when the darkness falls, and tucks you in,
pulling tight the edges, so that you won't fall.
A father, who simply wants to protect you,
guard you against the harshness of the day,
against the night, against the monsters hiding
in the dark corners.

I am so tired, alone, and scared.
I call out for your presence, just one last time.

I believe that some Great Power holds us softly,
that we can be cradled by the winds and
rocked back and forth, back and forth,
back, back to moments before the pain, before all the loss,
back when the shadows were monsters,
back, back to the night of childhood dreams,
back to when I could simply call out
and he would come, adjusting the covers
and my pillow so that my head lay gently
upon the darkness.

I believe in love.

I believe in the eternity of love, in holiness.
That breath and soul conspire and mingle
with the harshness and the softness,
the living and the gone.

I believe in grace,

and that some things don't die
and that most things cannot be explained.

And I know that when your father dies
your place in the universe shifts.

And like the night walk of the soul,
I will forever search the border for the gate that swings
open and shut, open and shut, open, open.

To the God of Mystery

We pray, we shout, we implore.
We are here, bereft and lost.
Help us use this sorrow for good.
We must not run, nor hide, nor deny our grief.

Make meaning out of our shattered hearts,
lest the fractures cripple us forever.

Create a sense of purpose
out of our desire for wholeness,
lest the repair we seek is mere vanity.

Grief has cast us into the Mystery.
There is so much we cannot comprehend.
Why the suffering? Why the loss?
Why did this happen?
Why?

Let us instead ask, what and how.
What can we learn from this pain and
how can we be of service?
May our questions open our hearts
that we may, in some small way,
ease the suffering of this complex life.

You Ask So Much
Kaddish

To the God of the bereaved.

Yitkadash.
May the sacred become
the vessel for my suffering.
Amen.

May I declare Your greatness
v'yitgadal and dwell in grandeur and
devotion, now, and forever.
Amen.

May I find comfort in this moment
of immense loss. *Sh'mei Raba.*
Your name is Great Abundance.
Amen.

Help me, O God of the mourner.
Comfort me.

May my grief open my heart
to compassion and understanding.
Amen.

This.
Only this.

Amen and amen.

Remember

Yizkor

We are compelled to remember. Today we cannot escape our mortality. We ask that mortality become our teacher. Uncertainty teaches us humility; ambiguity tempers our arrogance; and in the yielding to life's great mystery, we attain a measure of wisdom.

Yizkor. Every morning that we are granted another day of life, we are invited to the miracle of awakening. We are invited to awaken to the beauty of the universe, to awaken to possibility and abundance. To be awake to the daily miracles that are so terribly obvious and to which we are so often oblivious. We must not sleep. Let us accept the invitation to awaken our minds and spirits to the life that we have been granted, however small, however imperfect, however short.

Let our sorrow teach us compassion. Let our tears compel us to ease the pain of another. Let our sense of mortality make our lives stand for something great. When we love our neighbor, we transcend. When we love the stranger, we transcend. When we remove the obstacle before the blind, we transcend. When we pursue peace, we transcend. When we hold the world as a vessel of grace, we transcend. And behold, it is our bodies that enable us to walk through this world with hands that heal and arms that embrace and minds curious for understanding and solutions. We walk through this world with eyes that see possibility and ears that hear the voice of another and mouths that speak with benevolence. It is our physical nature that gives us the potential to enlighten and love and care. This is how we make life better, safer, stronger.

There is power in righteous acts. Compassion is the antidote for despair. Hope allows us to reach for eternity.

Yizkor. How powerful is the obligation to remember our dead. And how powerful do we become when we sustain moments of vulnerability, when we linger in fragility. How powerful is the human spirit that longs for meaning and purpose. That seeks to touch the edge of the sky. How powerful is the experience of transcendence. And faith? *Yizkor.* My flesh and my heart fail, but God is my heart's strength and my lot forever.

There is little more than this: one precious life where love is legacy and kindness is redemptive and creativity is immortality and memory is sacred.

Yizkor.

The Valley

The valley of the shadow of death is a tender place.
It is a place of questions and things unsaid.
And grace.
And love.
And depth.
And sadness.
My heart is open.
My breath is gentle.
I am tired and sleepless.
So I sit a while by the still waters
and You are with me.
God is with me.
I shall not fear.

ACTS OF VIOLENCE, WAR, AND NATURAL DISASTER

For Courage and Comfort

Be strong and let your heart have courage. (Psalm 31:25)

God, hear our prayer.

With horror we bear witness to
the evil within our midst.
We pray that our broken hearts
do not become embittered.
Let us not give in to cynicism and despair.
May we find comfort in our faith and in our community,
and may we strengthen our resolve
to be messengers of peace and healing,
bringing comfort to the broken-hearted.

We pray for the soul of our country.
May violence be no more.
May the way of our land be for good and not for evil.
May the words we speak, inspire.
May our outstretched arms, embrace.
May our minds learn tolerance and understanding.
Strike the inclination to do evil from
the hearts of the wicked.
Empower us for good, for life, for love.

God, we pray for the children.
The children, our greatest gift,
the hope in our hearts, the delight of lives,
our future and legacy.
The children, dear God.
Innocent and true.

Our children, pure in their beauty,
proof of goodness and miracle.
Our children, the children, dear God.
May we be strong and may our hearts have courage.

To the God of Doubt

Dear God, why?

Help us understand why
this eerie darkness falls upon daylight.
Smoke and ash. An unnatural silence,
then moaning, then sirens, then screams.
And shock. Disbelief. Anger. Sadness.

We cannot look away. We must not turn away.

Help us to have faith and courage
when there is confusion and doubt.

Give us the strength to look into the eyes of the wicked,
to be defiant and determined.
May we prevail.

May we have the resolve and wisdom to
bring safety to our broken and fractured world.

Dear God, bring healing to those in pain
and comfort to those bereaved.

You created this world from light and goodness.
You make peace in the high heavens.

Help us find the way to make peace here on earth.
God of doubt, hear our prayer.

A Prayer of Courage and Consolation

Holy One of Blessing,
grant us the will to stand firm
in the face of evil and hostility,
not to be silent or afraid.
To work diligently and faithfully
to banish wickedness from the earth.

Holy One of Blessing,
grant us the courage and resolve
to speak when there is hatred,
to act when there is confusion,
to join with others in building a world of safety,
understanding, and acceptance.

Because there is hate, dear God,
help us heal our fractured and broken world.

Because there is fear, dear God,
grant courage and faith to those in need.

Because there is pain, dear God,
bring healing to the shattered and wounded.

Because there is hope, dear God,
teach us to be a force for justice and kindness.

Because there is love, dear God,
help us to be a beacon of light and compassion.

As it is written:
Be strong and let your heart have courage. (Joshua 1:6)
Depart from evil, do good, seek peace and pursue it. (Psalm 34:15)

For the Children

God of the innocent.

What is this terror that has invaded our world?
We see a gray and awful shadow looming.
Don't tell us that monsters are real.

Hush, child, shhh.

Lay your head upon my heart, little one.
Feel the healing touch of my love.
If only I could suffer in your stead,
I, who am strong; you, a mere child.

Pray with me.

God, lift the pain and fear
from this tender life.

Grant us courage, miracle, healing,
and redemption from pain.

Guide the doctors,
may their wisdom and skill prevail.

May the compassion of the nurses
ease our fear and uncertainty.

God, of the innocent,
protect us.

Restore What Is Broken

In this time of uncertainty and fear
do not let me rest.
Send me forth that I may
restore what is broken,
heal what is wounded,
and engage in acts of love
with great and unrelenting determination.
I shall do something kind
and necessary for someone else.
May this be my answer to pain.

For Suffering

May I see the spark of holiness in all that I do.
May the light of God guide me through the darkness.

May my prayers strengthen me,
urging me to be present for those who are suffering.

May I become a messenger of caring and compassion,
a partner with God in the work of healing.

May I be guided to fight injustice
and to love peace and harmony.

May God's blessing be with those who are in my heart,
as I utter this prayer.

May all that is good in life lead me to passion and
radiance.

To the God of Creation

The earth shakes to the very foundations,
fire and water
unleashed
fury.

Creator of the universe,
whose name is love and compassion
and whose essence is wisdom, divinity, purpose.

We cry in anguish.
We are submerged in doubt and fear.
Help us to hold the suffering of the world
and offer a compassionate hand.

God of mercy,
be gentle with our pain and doubt.

Help us
as we struggle with confusion and loss.
Darkness, Cold. Fear. Hunger. Thirst.
Protect us.

Creator of the universe,
we offer gratitude
for the blessings, for survival,
for the graciousness of strangers,
and for heroic acts that abound.

Grant us strength, resilience, fortitude,
hope,
faith.

Prayers of Peace and Memorial

Light and Warmth

God,
may the passion of all that is good in life burn within my
heart.
My heart yearns for light and warmth.
May I be guided to feel fully and deeply,
fighting the injustice in the world while
loving peace and harmony.

By Your light, O God,
may I see light.

A Prayer for Nonviolence

God of life and Maker of all creation,
every act of violence in our world, in our communities,
and in our homes, destroys a part of Your creation.

Stir in our hearts a renewed sense of reverence for all life.

Give us the vision, the wisdom, and the courage
to create a community of safety for our children.

Guide us in Your ways so that we may
break the cycle of violence.

This we believe:
that peace, love, and healing begin with us.

Tonight, let us begin.
Amen.

Blessing for the Soldiers

Blessings upon the many
who run into danger,
whose inner strength and skill
put the safety of the stranger
above their own.

Protect those who serve,
who protect us from violence and war.

May their strength and courage
prevail over the forces
that plot against us.

May they stay safe and whole,
sound of body and spirit.
They seek only to serve
to protect.

Protect them.

A Prayer for Courage
In Time of War in Israel

Holy One of Blessing, we pray for the soldiers
who are called to defend the people of Israel.
Keep them safe.

When they are weary, give them strength.
When they are scared, give them courage.
May they find strength and faith in the days ahead.

Holy One of Blessing,
we pray for the people of Israel, who long to live
under Your canopy of peace.
Keep them safe.

When they are threatened, protect them from harm.
When they are wounded and bereaved, grant them healing
and comfort.
May they find strength and courage in the days ahead.

May our voices carry prayers of hope
that the people of Israel know that they are not alone.

Dear God, give us courage.
There is nothing more sacred than peace.

We Remember
For Those Who Serve and Defend

We stand with the families of the fallen
offering our gratitude, promising never to forget.

We pledge to tell the stories of courage, and the tales of
the valiant heart.
In quiet reverence, we hold their fear and pain and
sacrifice.
May the memory of their bravery be a precious legacy.

We stand with the families of the fallen
offering our gratitude, promising never to forget.

May God bless you and keep you.
May the light of God shine upon your darkened world.
May you be lifted and carried by your faith and
community.
May we work together for peace.

As we say,
amen.

Israel Memorial Day

Shaalu sh'lom Y'rushalayim,
We pray for the peace of Jerusalem,
may those who love you be at ease. (Psalm 122:6)

Shelter us, O Holy One,
as we wander the streets of Your holy city,
as we walk upon the mountains and valleys of the land.

We pray for the peace of Israel,
may those who care for you be at ease.

Guide us, O God,
as we search for the way to understanding
that our children should know laughter and tranquility.

We pray for the peace of our people everywhere,
may those who love them be at ease.

May compassion be our strength,
and the light of Torah be our guide,
and the song of hope be forever on our lips.
May we be a free people living in our land
under a canopy of eternal peace.
Peace.

Our Common Purpose

Prayers for Community and Assembly

Community comes from the word "common." The word assumes an awareness that we share in the most basic way: tears, loss, love, illness, joy, fear, birth, death, life. We are not meant to live alone. We are not supposed to ignore or deny what we have in common as human beings. That is the power of community. It is the acknowledgment of the universals of life, the sameness, the common ground. It is the knowledge that I will never be alone when I am sick; that I can share the mixed emotions I will have when my children go away to college; that when I pray for the secret desires of my soul, I will be joined by others doing the same. I live amid strangers, acquaintances, friends, and even a few people whom I don't like. What makes us a community is the sense of shared responsibility: when one is in need, the other simply responds.

The Call to Service

In the presence of God,
the Creator and Sustainer of life;

with reverence to our Torah,
holy with wisdom and insight;

and with the consent of our community,
vibrant and growing;

we know that you have been called to service,
and we ask that you lovingly and faithfully bear this
responsibility.

May God be with you, guiding your path,
inspiring you and enriching your lives.

May your service be one of meaning and grace,
achievement and success.

May you grow in wisdom, conviction, and Jewish
learning.

May you honor our heritage
while embracing the evolving traditions of our people.

May the Holy One grant you the clear vision, faith, and
courage
to carry forward the values of our congregation.

May this prayer be for the blessing for all.

The Covenant of Leadership

May we serve our congregation
With humility and strength,
With vision and an empathetic ear,
With passion and compassion,
And to labor not for personal gain but for the vitality of
Our congregation and the Jewish people.

We take upon ourselves a covenant of leadership,
That we may become worthy heirs
of those who came before us
and discerning and patient leaders,
searching for the ones who will succeed us.

The Leadership Pledge

To be a leader you must have humility
and ask for guidance.

To be a leader you must have courage
and step forward bravely into the future.

To be a leader you must have faith,
faith in God, faith in the goodness of people, and faith in
the future.

To be a leader you must have vision and optimism,
seeing into the future with excitement and hope.

To be a leader you must be kind.
You must listen.

You must be ethical and act out of conviction.

You must work together
and empower others to lead.

You must never act out of fear
and you must be brave.

A Blessing for Our Community

May our synagogue be a vibrant
and holy place.

A place where people join together
to learn and to contemplate,

to be kind and to be purposeful,
to be silent and to be energetic,

to be forgiving and to be loving,
to understand commandment and obligation,

to work for peace, freedom,
and prosperity in a broken world,

to find faith and be guided
on a journey of the spirit.

May our synagogue be a vibrant and holy place
so that we may be strengthened by God,
community, and acts of loving-kindness.

Hear Our Prayer
For the Women of the Wall

It is not the sound of triumph
Or the sound of the melody of defeat.
It is the sound of song that I hear.

What did this people do? (Exodus 32:18, 32:21)

The stones of the ancient wall stand strong
from touch, from tears, from the hope of our people.
We offer prayers of longing, prayers of peace,
of gladness, of healing, of gratitude.

The ageless sounds of supplication.
Hear O Israel,
Listen.

In the distance the voices of our women,
powerful and steadfast, as it is written:
Sing a new song unto God. (Psalm 96:1)

The voices of our men,
mighty and resolved, as it is written:
Worship God in the beauty of holiness. (Psalm 96:9)

The sound of supplication.
Hear O Israel,
Listen.

To the sound of the shofar, *t'kiah g'dolah*,
a mighty blast, sustained with anticipation,
yearning and expectation.

Holy One of Blessing, guide us in our struggle.
Grant us wisdom and discernment as we search
for the path of freedom and righteousness.

Honor and majesty are before God,
strength and beauty in God's sanctuary. (Psalm 96:6)

Hear our prayer.

A Prayer for an Assembly

There is power in assembly.
We have assembled to bear witness
to goodness and compassion and
to claim a vision of wholeness and peace.

O God, grant us peace.

There is power in meeting.
When we assemble in holy convocation,
we recall the Tent of Meeting,
where God's presence is called upon
for guidance and direction.

O God, be our guide.

We live in difficult and troubled times.
We sing of peace as some move toward war.

May we find the wisdom and determination
to fight evil, pursue justice, and seek peace.

There is power in assembly.
We meet in prayer to bring hope to a broken world;
we call on light to expel the darkness,
we ask for guidance as we confront danger.

O God, God of all creation, grant us wisdom,
discernment, courage, and vision.
Bless this sacred assembly.

A Prayer for a Community Gathering

As we gather in thoughtful deliberation,
may we be inspired with

hope,
that we may stay strong and resilient,

with wisdom,
that we may discern the path for our community,

with vision,
that we may see what is possible,

with courage,
that we may step into our future,

with a passion for justice,
that we may nurture and heed the righteous among us,

with a yearning for peace,
that we may manifest well-being and wholeness.

A Prayer for Justice and Democracy

Chein v'chesed, beauty and grace:
this is a historic moment of courage and vision,
this is a holy convocation.

Chein v'chesed, beauty and grace:
when we stand together, it is holy;
and when we raise our voices in song, there is
transcendence;
and when we pray, there is joy.

Chein v'chesed, beauty and grace:
When we plead the case of the oppressed, there is justice.
As Huldah the prophet said, *your heart is tender unto God.*
(2 Kings 22:19)
And as Miriam commanded, *sing unto God a song of
triumph.* (Exodus 15:21)

Chein v'chesed v'rachamin, beauty, grace, and love:
We have joined together to be counted,
to be present, to be known, and to be named.

May we go from strength to strength.

May our work bring the sacred down to earth,
may we instill joy into the hearts of all men and women,
and may we offer songs and hymns of gratitude.

We come together to celebrate our freedoms and the
democracy that we so cherish.
As it is written in the prophet Isaiah:
*Widen the place of your tents, stretch forth the curtains, lengthen
the cords, and strengthen the stakes.* (Isaiah 54:2)

A Convocation for an Interfaith Gathering

May this assembly become a tent large enough to welcome people of differing opinions and diverse voices.

This is a forum of honest and sincere inquiry. We enter into debate and conversation to learn and discern the possibilities for the leadership of our country. Democracy is a sacred right, and voting a hallowed obligation.

On this we agree and for this we pray:

We ask for faith. May we turn our prayers into action. All peoples should live free of fear. We search for ways to pursue acts of kindness, helping to heal those whose lives are broken.

We ask for courage. May we ever stand strong with the righteous of all peoples, pursuing peace and working for justice.

We ask for wisdom. May our voices become a choir of hope in a dangerous world and our deeds a beacon of light where there is darkness.

As it is written in the Book of Isaiah: *In righteousness shall you be established: you shall be far from oppression, for you shall not fear; and terror shall not come near you.* (Isaiah 54:14)

And so, as we begin, we pray for faith, courage, and wisdom.

The Psalm of the Day

There is a Jewish tradition to recite a prescribed psalm for each day of the week. These daily psalms are a part of the morning liturgical offering. Some traditions divide the Book of Psalms, 150 psalms in all, into seven sections. Each day, a section is read as a type of devotional, helping to focus and ground the heart and mind in poetic and prayerful text.

The following seven psalms are based on the traditional texts. While composing them, I dialogued with the psalm, going in and out of my voice and the voice of the psalmist. I used two different translations, depending on the psalm. Translation is interpretation, and I found myself inspired by both the New JPS translation and the rendering in Richard N. Levy's book *Songs of Ascending: The Book of Psalms; A New Translation* (CCAR Press). There is a note at the end of this volume signifying which translation is used.

The psalms speak to the depth of human experience, helping us find the words for longing, courage, fear, and faith. They offer gratitude and wonder; implore God to be delivered from the hand of the enemy; express despair and confusion. Over the centuries a book of psalms has been carried in the pocket of a soldier going onto the battlefield and in the hand of a woman in labor entering into the delivery room.

They are the companion to our spirit.

To God of the Heights: Lift Me

SUNDAY: *Psalm 24*

A child walks upon the mist-filled clearing,
white flowers scattered upon the green.

In the distance the mountaintop is covered with
a cloud that has fallen, truth is all in haze.

Who shall ascend to the mountain of Adonai
and who shall stand at Your sacred site?

Open my hand, extend my hand, I reach
toward the God of intention,

for I am but a child, afraid, aware, unaware.

Open my heart, O Lovely One, that I may know
the whole earth is filled with Your Glory.

Raise up your heads, O regal gates—
Let yourselves be raised up, O doors to eternity!
Let there enter the Ruler of Glory!

And I will climb, and behold and stand in awe
upon the summit and gaze upon the beauty.

Beauty and blessing abound.
Selah.

To the God of War and Peace: Prevail
MONDAY: *Psalm 48*

We live within,
crowded by a multitude of voices
benevolent and violent, sure and insecure,
and pained and caring and oh so critical.

Sometimes conflicting voices wage war
upon our being.
Cacophony, clamor, and discord resound,
our inner peace and quiet, supplanted, banished.

See, the kings joined forces;
they advanced together.
At the mere sight of it they were stunned,
they were terrified, they panicked;
they were seized there with a trembling.

God of quiet mercies, prevail
upon my inner tendencies for strife.
I place my trust in a Greater Good!
Break the bonds of the wounded heart;
release me from my prison of pain.

Come and see what the God of mercies has done,
The Holy One puts a stop to wars throughout the earth,
breaking the bow, snapping the spear, consigning wagons to the flames.

The God of hosts is with us; the God of Jacob is our haven.
Selah.

We have meditated on Your love, God,
in the heart of Your sanctuary.

I surrender to my awareness of You.
In my heart, a sanctuary of love.
Amen. Selah.

To the Judge of All the Earth: Advocate

TUESDAY: Psalm 82

A thin layer surrounds my heart and I am protected.
Protected against visions of pain and violence.
Protected against sounds of crying.
Protected. And blinded to suffering.

How many are invisible to my compassion?
They go about in darkness; all the foundations of the earth totter.

God stands in the divine assembly;
among the divine beings God pronounces judgment.

Hold the forgotten and the orphan,
vindicate the lowly and the poor,
rescue the unseen and the needy;
save them from the hand of the wicked.

God of judgment, judge me.
Confound my complacency.
Agitate my illusions, enlist me
and I shall join the Assembly of the Divine.

To the God of Peace: Save Us
WEDNESDAY: *Psalm 94*

Are You not the One
who is Good and Beauty, Creator of all things?
Why did You give us the choice between good and evil?
Why do we repeatedly choose the way of iniquity?

Adversity assails us, we are surrounded by wicked intent.
Our enemies sing songs of war.
Save us from dismay and destruction.

All the doers of iniquity act boastfully.
They crush Your people, Adonai.

When will You rise up,
and give rest from days of suffering?

How long shall the wicked exult?
Give rest from days of suffering.

We seek refuge in Your goodness;
lift us upon the bedrock of strength and righteousness.

May our hearts be brave.
May we stand firm in our pursuit of justice.
May the drums of war become the heartbeat of peace.

To the God of Creation: A Song of Thanks

THURSDAY: *Psalm 81*

I pray.

I fall to my knees, my back arches
lifting my face toward the heavens.

I embrace the space between.
My heart opens with joy.

We are mere children of God,
small, exuberant, infused with love.

The mountain of God shows me the path to ascend.
The sunlight is ember red within my lids.
The cold mountain air lingers, frost grips the land,
the chill stings my cheeks.
Boulders of limestone share the mountainside with wild
sage and hyssop.

God of wonder. God of beauty. God of complexity.
God of simplicity.

How do we forget the song of holiness?
Remember, all you children of God.
Remember.

Let joyful song ring out to God, our strength,
Ring out t'ruah to the God of Jacob!

Raise a song, celebrate on the drum,
a lyre and a lute making sweet harmonies
together!

Remember all you children of God.
Remember.
The world is love.
Sing a song of
love.

To the Center of the Universe: A Yielding
FRIDAY: Psalm 93

I surrender.
I surrender all delusion of control.
I surrender.
I surrender all sense of self at the center.
I surrender.
I surrender my need to know the unknowable.
I surrender.
I surrender the urge to be the conductor of all things,
of other people's lives, of my own life.
I surrender.

And in this yielding of the spirit, I am no longer alone.
To be in the center of my world is to be in a lonely place.

God,
You,
The Center,
The Marrow of Life,
The Ruling Principle of the universe,
The Transcendent Power.
Tether me to something grand, to eternity, to awe and beauty.

God is supreme, robed in grandeur;
God is robed, girded with strength.
The world stands firm; it cannot be shaken.

Take from me this need to know;
I enter into Your mysteries, a faithful servant.

Take from me this need to be right;
I enter into the ambiguities with a grateful heart.

Take from me this need for power;
I enter into the world, humble and stripped of illusion.

To the Center of the universe, Ruling Power of the universe,
I yield.

A Song of Gratitude: Open My Heart
THE SABBATH: Psalm 92

My open heart
is grateful, and broken, and strong.

I sing a song of praise when goodness is all around.

It is good to praise God,
to sing hymns to Your name, O Most High,

to proclaim Your steadfast love at daybreak,
Your faithfulness each night.

Teach me a song of praise,
when I lay crushed and depleted.
Let me raise my voice in gratitude
when I lose my way, when I am defeated.

This is the practice, O God of hosts.
To awaken every morning in gratitude,
when life is good, when life is hard,
when the spirit is strong,
when the heart is shaking with doubt.

An open heart
is grateful, and broken, and strong.
Teach me a song of praise.

Focus Phrases

THE IMAGES AND THOUGHTS that flow through our minds are unending and sometimes relentless. They can be positive, hopeful, encouraging, and affirming. And they can be shadow thoughts reinforcing fear, negativity, and an attitude of scarcity.

With intention, practice, and patience, we can elevate our thoughts and become the person we desire to be. The repetition of certain phrases can be a powerful tool in that process—a focus phrase verse either from a traditional text or of our own composition.

These phrases are devotionals. Through thoughtful and intentional recitation of a verse we are inspired to nurture a loving presence of hope, positivity, equanimity, and generosity.

This verse or phrase becomes a companion, accompanying us for weeks, months, or even years as we evolve. The repetitive recitation of the phrases helps us with seven practices: centering, reframing, affirmation, concentration, contemplation, cultivation, and discernment. These practices can lead us to be more self-aware and reflective. They foster a deeper sense of meaning, well-being, and connection.

Centering

How often do we use the following phrases: *I feel so scattered*; *I just need to collect my thoughts*; *my mind is jumping from thing to thing*; *I feel frantic and overwrought*? Focus phrases help us find our center. Centering is a practice that grounds us, makes us more conscious of our place in the world, and helps us make choices with greater intention.

Reframing

The way we tell our story impacts the way in which we see life. When we tell our story in negative tones and vocabulary, it is very hard to have a positive outlook and hopeful sense of being. We also may find that we experience fearful and negative self-talk. We may not be aware of how often we think in unconstructive and damaging ways. Focus phrases can help us re-record those negative tapes and shift us toward a more positive and loving way of thinking.

Affirmation

Affirmations sometimes feel dishonest. If we are imbedded with negative self-images of ourselves, offering an affirmation like *I am worthy of love* may feel false and uncomfortable and be very difficult to say. And yet, when we affirm the person we long to be, we foster new attitudes and perspectives. Focus phrases are affirmations of our higher self.

Concentration

When we sit in meditation, follow our breath, we settle in, drop in to ourselves. We quiet down and move away from a scattered and random way of being. We connect to our essential selves, our place in the world, and may even feel more connected with the transcendent sacred force of the universe.

Contemplation

How often do we merely stay a while and linger in thought and reflection? Intentional thinking is a practice, a habit. Reflective reading of sacred and inspirational texts, reflective writing or journaling, quiet consideration of ideas, and fostering compassion and forgiveness are each ways of creating a pathway, a safe container in which we can evolve and unfold. Focus phrases can be the opening for this practice.

Cultivation

It is possible to create new habits of thinking and behaving, develop our moral and spiritual character, foster positive relationships, and enhance the quality of our conversation. Focus phrases begin to help us build a container, a context, in which we can cultivate an elevated way of living and being, developing a positive and supportive environment for our growth, create a fertile field to consider, reframe, and expand our thinking.

Discernment

When we settle down, focus, and enter into quiet, we can discern the way of our evolving path. We seek guidance and learn to sharpen and trust our intuition. We are being called to a greater manifestation of our spiritual life. Focus phrases help us discern that calling.

The following section is divided into six subsections: finding meaning, guidance, self-love, forgiveness, positive energy, and courage. Each one of these topics is foundational as we try to find our true place in the world and to be settled in our hearts. In each subsection there are several offerings for a focus phrase. On every page an original phrase is coupled with a scriptural text. These are suggestions. Use them as is, or take them as a draft to refine for your own purpose.

Meaning is the inner question of the night:
why am I here?
Purpose is the external conversation we have with others:
I am here to help.

I offer an open heart, a deep breath. Help me hear.

The soul You have given me is pure.
  —From the morning liturgy, *Elohai N'shamah*

I shall go to the edge of what I know and sit a while.

A river flows from Eden to water the Garden.
  —Genesis 2:10

I am willing to step into my life.

I become a prayer to You, O God, the moment I am willing.
  —From the morning liturgy, *Elohai N'shamah*

What am I supposed to learn from this?

Holy. Holy. Holy.
  —Isaiah 6:3

GUIDANCE

Sometimes you chase your destiny,
and sometimes your destiny chases you.

Everything happens in God's time, and God is never late.

My soul is quiet, awaiting God.
—Psalm 62:2

I shall remain steadfast.

Though I have fallen, I rise again; though I sit in darkness,
God is my light.
—Micah 7:8

I choose hope over cynicism.

From the depths I call out to God.
—Psalm 130:1

Self-Love

Whatever the question, love is the answer.

The opposite of judgment is curiosity.

The world is held like a vessel of grace.
—From the daily liturgy, the *Amidah*

I want to be different once I emerge.

Lift yourself up! Shake off the dust. Array yourself in beauty.
—From the *Kabbalat Shabbat* liturgy, *L'chah Dodi*

Hold space.

By day God is kindness, by night God's song is with me.
—Psalm 42:9

I stand in grace and beauty.

I search for You, my soul thirsts for You.
—Psalm 63:2

Forgiveness is the gift you give yourself
when you choose to live in light rather than in darkness.

I choose love over fear.

Your kindness is before my eyes, and I have followed Your truth.
—Psalm 26:3

I am emboldened by beauty, diminished by judgment.

May I find grace in the wilderness.
—Jeremiah 31:2

My brokenness is not an excuse for bad behavior.

The stone that has been rejected by the builders is used as the main cornerstone.
—Psalm 118:22

I am ready to learn another way.

*You have dwelt long enough in the valley of tears;
now God will shower you with mercy.*
—From the *Kabbalat Shabbat* liturgy, *L'chah Dodi*

Positive Energy

Positivity is a matter of perspective. Shift. And again.

The light within is a gift to be nurtured.

Awake, awake, your light has come! Arise, shine, awake and sing!
   —From the *Kabbalat Shabbat* liturgy, *L'chah Dodi*

I accept the path of my life with kindness and compassion.

The path of the righteous is like radiant splendor.
   —Proverbs 4:18

Practice graciousness.

God redeems my soul in wholeness.
   —Psalm 55:19

I have been called to bear witness.

Creation is renewed daily, with goodness.
   —From the morning liturgy, *Yotzeir Or*

COURAGE

It takes courage to unfold, to step into your destiny.
It takes courage to become the hero of your life.
It takes courage to love another, to trust and enter into
vulnerabilities.

It takes courage to be.

Pull me, and I shall follow.

I am pursued by goodness and mercy all the days of my life.
—Psalm 23:6

I will become the hero of my life.

In quietness and confidence shall be your strength.
—Isaiah 30:15

I am always at the edge of the wilderness, sometimes entering, sometimes leaving.

Look toward God. Be strong and may your heart have courage.
—Psalm 27:14

With faith, I am never alone.

Come, let us consider together.
—Isaiah 1:18

SECTION VI
Questions

Playing Catch with the Universe

WHEN WE ARE YOUNG we are taught that no question is a bad question. While that may be true, in the world of spiritual development, some questions are better than others.

"Questioning" is a methodology in spiritual transformation. Asking questions is a skill, an art, a craft that can propel us on a path of greater awareness and discernment. Within the word "question" is the word "quest." A good question sets us on a quest; it is a good companion who accompanies us for a long while. It propels our journey. A good question can be become the defining principle of our character, our evolution, and the basis for our latest iteration of self.

Once we refine the question, we toss it out to the universe without any expectation or regard to an answer. We simply ask what we want to know. We linger in the question. Linger. And then, without fail, an answer comes to us. Days later, years later, hours later. In the line at the pharmacy, while taking a shower, in a dream one night, in the most random and unrelated way, the answer comes. Sometimes as a phrase or word, sometimes in a conversation with a friend or a stranger, sometimes in a deep knowing while driving quickly by a field heavy with morning frost. But it comes. And things begin to shift. Because a good question transports us to the next station in our journey.

In the following pages, I offer questions you may want to consider. I have organized them into three categories: faith, courage, and wisdom. These categories are like vessels that hold spiritual meaning: faith is the acknowledgment that we are in partnership with mystery; courage reflects the audacity, tenacity, and resilience that it takes to live fully; wisdom is a deep and abiding knowing that evolves in the spirit with the passage of time.

With every good question, a new layer of meaning and purpose unfolds.

FAITH

What is the question your life has been trying to answer?

What is my inner voice telling me?

Where can I find my inner calm?

Do I live in abundance or scarcity?

How do I practice discernment?

What is the source of my strength?

Am I willing?

What if I lived with the imperative of love?

What does it mean to live with ambiguity?

What do I need to understand?

How can I learn to trust?

What?

What does it mean to say yes?

What do I need to let go?

How can I be less fear based?

What prevents me?

What am I passionate about?

Courage

If I were to say yes, what would change?

If I let go of the emptiness, what would happen?

What is one next positive step I can take?

How can I manifest my best self?

What would it take to live with less fear?

What would have to change, to my make my life a prayer to God?

Am I determined or scared?

Where?

Who do I need to forgive?

What has to change for me to become resilient?

How can I replace judgment with curiosity?

Is this person or situation life affirming or life draining?

If I release the negative, what good awaits?

How shall I slay the beast?

What needs to be said? To whom?

What can I learn from the agitator in my life?

How can I manifest my greatest desire?

WISDOM

What support do I need to become me?

What is the great question of my life?

How?

What does my boredom reveal?

What is the source of my good?

Who am I pretending to be?

What negative forces prevail in my life?

What is it that I want to know?

Is my life balanced between giving and receiving?

How do I shift my perspective?

What is this obstacle teaching me?

Why does my life lack meaning?

Who are the sustainers in my life?

What do I want to know?

What is my sacred obligation?

How can I be more me?

Patience?

Notes

p. 15 Kedar, Karyn D., "Whispers" from *Bridge to Forgiveness: Stories and Prayers for Finding God and Restoring Wholeness* (Woodstock, VT: Jewish Lights, 2011).

p. 19 Kedar, Karyn D., "Quiet My Soul, O Holy One" from *Bridge to Forgiveness: Stories and Prayers for Finding God and Restoring Wholeness* (Woodstock, VT: Jewish Lights, 2011).

p. 20 "Diving into the Wreck" is the title poem of the book by Adrienne Rich, 1973.

p. 22 Kedar, Karyn D., "Learning" from *Bridge to Forgiveness: Stories and Prayers for Finding God and Restoring Wholeness* (Woodstock, VT: Jewish Lights, 2011).

p. 23 Kedar, Karyn D., "Decide" from *Omer: A Counting* (New York, NY: CCAR Press, 2014).

p.32 Kedar, Karyn D., "Learning to Yield" From *Bridge to Forgiveness: Stories and Prayers for Finding God and Restoring Wholeness* (Woodstock, VT: Jewish Lights, 2011).

p. 42 Kedar, Karyn D., "Choosing" from *Bridge to Forgiveness: Stories and Prayers for Finding God and Restoring Wholeness* (Woodstock, VT: Jewish Lights, 2011).

p. 45 Kedar, Karyn D., "Hope is the Bridge" from *God Whispers: Stories of the Soul, Lessons of the Heart* (Woodstock, VT: Jewish Lights, 2001).

p. 47 Kedar, Karyn D., "The Ghost of Love" from *Bridge to Forgiveness: Stories and Prayers for Finding God and Restoring Wholeness* (Woodstock, VT: Jewish Lights, 2011).

p. 50 Kedar, Karyn D., "Guide Me" from *Omer: A Counting* (New York, NY: CCAR Press, 2014).

p. 54 Kedar, Karyn D., "My Rock" from *Bridge to Forgiveness: Stories and Prayers for Finding God and Restoring Wholeness* (Woodstock, VT: Jewish Lights, 2011).

p. 56   Kedar, Karyn D., "Perpetual Crossings" from *Bridge to Forgiveness: Stories and Prayers for Finding God and Restoring Wholeness* (Woodstock, VT: Jewish Lights, 2011).

p. 59   Kedar, Karyn D., "Courage" from *Omer: A Counting* (New York, NY: CCAR Press, 2014).

p. 62   Kedar, Karyn D., "Life Defined" from *Bridge to Forgiveness: Stories and Prayers for Finding God and Restoring Wholeness* (Woodstock, VT: Jewish Lights, 2011).

p. 64   Kedar, Karyn D., "Discern" from *Omer: A Counting* (New York, NY: CCAR Press, 2014).

p. 66   Kedar, Karyn D., "Forgiveness" from *Bridge to Forgiveness: Stories and Prayers for Finding God and Restoring Wholeness* (Woodstock, VT: Jewish Lights, 2011).

p. 69   Kedar, Karyn D., "The Truth" *God Whispers: Stories of the Soul, Lessons of the Heart* (Woodstock, VT: Jewish Lights, 2001).

p. 70   Kedar, Karyn D., "Hope, Banish My Despair" from *Omer: A Counting* (New York, NY: CCAR Press, 2014).

p. 83   Kedar, Karyn D., "Imagination" from *Omer: A Counting* (New York, NY: CCAR Press, 2014).

p. 97   Kedar, Karyn D., "I Lift My Eyes" *Bridge to Forgiveness: Stories and Prayers for Finding God and Restoring Wholeness* (Woodstock, VT: Jewish Lights, 2011).

p. 99   Kedar, Karyn D., "Learning from Death" from *God Whispers: Stories of the Soul, Lessons of the Heart* (Woodstock, VT: Jewish Lights, 2001).

p. 100   Kedar, Karyn D., "From a Mother to Her Girls" from *Bridge to Forgiveness: Stories and Prayers for Finding God and Restoring Wholeness* (Woodstock, VT: Jewish Lights, 2011).

p. 106   "Remember" by Kedar, Karyn D. excerpt from "Ode to Mortality" in *May God Remember: Memory and Memorializing in Judaism*, ed. Rabbi Lawrence A. Hoffman (Woodstock, VT: Jewish Lights, 2013), pp. 175–177.

p. 117 Kedar, Karyn D., "On Suffering" from *Omer: A Counting* (New York, NY: CCAR Press, 2014).

p. 121 Kedar, Karyn D., "Light and Warmth" from *Bridge to Forgiveness: Stories and Prayers for Finding God and Restoring Wholeness* (Woodstock, VT: Jewish Lights, 2011).

p. 128 Kedar, Karyn D., "Community" from *God Whispers: Stories of the Soul, Lessons of the Heart* (Woodstock, VT: Jewish Lights, 2001).

p. 141 The Psalm 24 text in italics is from the translation by Rabbi Richard Levy, in *Songs Ascending*.

p. 142 The Psalm 48 text in italics is from the translation of Psalm 48 by Rabbi Richard Levy, in *Songs Ascending*, and adapted from the JPS translation of Psalms 46 and 48.

p. 143 The Psalm 82 text in italics is adapted from the JPS translation.

p. 144 The Psalm 94 text in italics is from the translation by Rabbi Richard Levy, in *Songs Ascending*.

p. 145 The Psalm 81 text in italics is from the translation by Rabbi Richard Levy, in *Songs Ascending*.

p. 146 The Psalm 93 text in italics is adapted from the JPS translation.

p. 148 The Psalm 92 text in italics is adapted from the JPS translation.

RABBI KARYN D. KEDAR is the senior rabbi at Congregation BJBE in the Chicago area. Her previously published books include *God Whispers*, *The Dance of the Dolphin (Our Dance with God)*, *The Bridge to Forgiveness*, and *Omer: A Counting*. She is published in numerous anthologies and is renowned for her creative liturgy. Rabbi Kedar teaches courses and leads retreats that explore the need for meaning and purpose in our busy lives, creating an intentional life, spiritual awakening, forgiveness, as well as inspirational leadership and creating the synagogue for the twenty-first century.

Printed in the USA
CPSIA information can be obtained
at www.ICGtesting.com
CBHW060015090924
14261CB00014B/1239